Beautiful America's San Diego

Cabrillo National Monument

Published by
Beautiful America Publishing Company©
P.O. Box 646
Wilsonville, Oregon 97070

Design: Jacelen Pete
Linotronic output: LeFont Laser Imaging

Library of Congress Catalog Number 92-42559

ISBN 0-89802-629-6
ISBN 0-89802-632-6 (Paperback)

Printed in Korea

Beautiful America's

San Diego

Photography by Ken Naversen

Text by Andrea Naversen

Beautiful America Publishing Company

Contents

Foreword

I'm a wanderer at heart, a vagabond. My brothers and I grew up all over the United States, as the children of an Air Force officer and his wife. One year here. Two years there. In big towns and little towns. The constant moves gave me a sense of independence (being the new kid on the playground will do that to you), and a curiosity for what lay beyond my own backyard.

And so, as a print journalist, and later as a television reporter, my wanderings continued. Three years here. Four years there. In big towns and little towns.

I'm still a wanderer at heart, but one now with roots firmly planted in San Diego. This is finally home. It's not just the weather that keeps me here, although warm, beautiful days year round do tend to spoil you. It's not just the blue Pacific breaking a few miles from my door. And it's not just the wealth of things to do, whether it's a day on the beach or a night at the Old Globe.

What keeps me here is San Diego's sense of community. It's a big town, but somehow it has managed to retain its small town feel. You know your neighbors here. You belong. San Diego is sort of like the bar in the TV show "Cheers." It's a warm, familiar place. Here, everybody knows your name. Or maybe it just feels that way.

Embarcadero and boat harbor, San Diego Bay

(Opposite) Skyline at sunset

San Diego

I thought San Diego must be a heaven on earth, if it was all as fine as that. It seemed to me the best spot for building a city I ever saw.

Alonzo Horton is still right after all these years. On April 15, 1867, he first set eyes on San Diego. And he liked what he saw—San Diego Bay, the peninsula that would later be called Coronado Island, the long spit of land known as Point Loma. The father of San Diego had found his heaven on earth. Horton went on to build what is now the sixth largest city in the country: 1.15 million people in the city, 2.6 million in the county.

San Diego is a Navy town, home of one of the largest and busiest naval ports in the world. Many of the Pacific Fleet's carriers, cruisers, destroyers, and submarines are stationed here. Navy ships sail in and out of San Diego Harbor, and F-14 Tomcats from Miramar's Fighter Town USA soar through its skies.

It's also a science town—world famous research facilities are located here, including the Salk Institute, the Scripps Research Institute, and the La Jolla Cancer Research Foundation. San Diego is also home to a burgeoning high-tech/biotech industry. It has the fourth largest concentration of biotechnology companies in the country, with more than one hundred headquartered here.

It's a sports town—home to the Padres, the Chargers, the champion Sockers, as well as recent host to the America's Cup, sailing's biggest prize. But San Diegans aren't content just to watch, they join in: jogging, surfing, cycling, and rollerblading on the boardwalks.

And San Diego, of course, is a resort town, with seventy miles of sand and surf stretching all the way from the Mexican border to the beach communities of the North County. There are more than two dozen beaches here, each with its own distinct personality: from Mission Beach, where the summer seems endless (and so do the parties), to La Jolla Cove, a paradise for snorkelers. And where else can you find an average seventy-degree temperature year round? No wonder San Diego's reputation is spreading abroad as a world-class tourist destination.

San Diego is home to such famous attractions as Sea World and the San Diego Zoo and Wild Animal Park. Balboa Park is a cultural center with its many museums, including the San Diego Museum of Art, and theatres such as the Old Globe. Adding to the city's rich cultural life are the San Diego Symphony, Opera, Repertory Theatre, the Museum of Contemporary Art, and the La Jolla Playhouse.

Downtown

Now known as "America's Finest City," San Diego was envisioned by Alonzo Horton, a merchant from San Francisco who arrived here aboard the steamer *Pacific*. In her book on Horton, Elizabeth C. MacPhail writes, "He was asked where he thought the city should be. 'Right down there by the wharf. I have been nearly all over the United States and that is the prettiest place for a city I ever saw. Is there any land for sale?'" There was.

Horton bought up 960 acres at auction for $265—a real bargain at about twenty-seven-and-a-half cents an acre—and San Diego's downtown was born. But the San Diego Historical Society says Horton had to shell out an additional $4,000 two years later for a single parcel to complete his New Town. By some oversight, he missed the lot. And by the time Horton realized it, the land had soared in value.

At first, folks were skeptical that Horton's hopes for a city weren't just another "Davis's Folly." William Heath Davis, a merchant and trader, had tried to build a town on the same spot seventeen years earlier. But Horton succeeded where Davis had failed.

Despite the eventual success of his New Town, Horton died a poor man, most of his property lost through tax sales and foreclosures. But on his ninety-fifth birthday he told a newspaper reporter that the city he helped build was still "the most beautiful place in the world." If he were alive today, Horton would probably feel the same way.

Nowhere is the city's growth more evident than downtown, where gleaming office towers climb the horizon, their mirrored glass reflecting both sea and sky.

There are many fine hotels here, from the venerable U.S. Grant, built in 1910, with its elegant marble lobby (have a drink in the warm, wood-paneled Grant Grill Lounge) to the posh new

Convention Center

Aerial view of Convention Center and marina

Pan Pacific where East meets West. Along the marina, the Marriott's twin glass towers glitter and the New Hyatt Regency scrapes the sky. Nearby, the San Diego Convention Center looks like a great ship ready to set sail.

From there, it's a short stroll along the boardwalk to Seaport Village with fourteen acres of shopping and entertainment. There are more than sixty-five shops, and four restaurants, many with views of San Diego Bay. For a quick snack, you can choose from a number of eateries. Dine at tables outside or carry your picnic to a grassy spot overlooking the water and the Navy ships moored nearby. There's even a restored 1890 carousel, transplanted from Coney Island, for big and little kids alike.

Seaport Village is located at 849 West Harbor Drive at Kettner Boulevard.

Close by on the Embarcadero is the Maritime Museum, at 1300 N. Harbor Drive. Here you can tour a trio of ships: the famous *Star of India*, which dates to 1863, the oldest iron-hulled sailing ship still afloat; the 1898 ferryboat *Berkeley*; and the 1904 steam yacht *Medea*, the epitome of yachting luxury at the turn of the century.

If you feel like taking a boat ride after your tour, catch a ferry to Coronado Island from the Broadway Pier, or take one and two-hour harbor excursions around San Diego Bay.

In the heart of the city is Horton Plaza, a $140 million project which helped to revitalize downtown, turning a decaying business district into a center for both commercial and residential development.

The plaza is a sort of open-air urban bazaar, with colorful banners, topiary animals, and a turn-of-the-century clock. Here you'll find pushcart vendors, street musicians, and mimes.

This multi-level mall stretches for nearly seven city blocks with more than 140 shops, galleries, and restaurants; a seven-screen cinema; and the Lyceum Theatre for performing arts. On the top level, there's an international food fair, where you can grab a quick bite at many ethnic eateries. On Restaurant Row, the pace is more leisurely. Choose from the California Cafe Bar & Grill, Pagliacci Trattoria, the Panda Inn, and others. On the bottom level is the Farmer's Market, actually a fancy supermarket with fresh bread and gourmet fare. And for a place to stay, just steps from all this shopping and dining, there's the Doubletree Hotel adjacent to the plaza.

Horton Plaza's award-winning design is eclectic, borrowing from Spanish Colonial, Mediterranean, Gothic, and other styles. But the colors are pure California: peach, terra cotta, yellow, and mauve. The plaza's architectural design is the work of Jon Jerde, who designed the 1984 Los Angeles Olympic Games.

Horton Plaza is located between Broadway and G Street, and First and Fourth avenues, next to the Gaslamp Quarter.

Next door is the Paladion—a $34 million retail center that has brought the upscale to downtown. It's ritzy. It's glitzy. It's San Diego's answer to Rodeo Drive. Some of the fanciest stores in the world are all gathered under one glittering roof: Tiffany, Cartier, Ferragamo, Gucci, Nina Ricci, Gianni Versace, Alfred Dunhill. You name it. It's probably here. And how's this for pampering? There's even valet parking.

The Paladion is filled with peach-tinted mirrors (selected to flatter a woman's complexion), Italian marble, polished brass, and fine wood. Shops are arranged on three levels around the central Ivy Court where you'll find not only ladies who lunch, but busy executives. The restaurant also serves coffee and pastries in the morning, high tea in the afternoon, cocktails and after-theatre fare at night. Take the escalator to the plaza level for lunch or dinner at Bice Ristorante. Or pop into the Spa de la Mer to relax and rejuvenate after spending all that money. It offers the works, including facials, massage, and hydrotherapy treatments.

Too rich for your blood? Retailers insist there's something for everyone here. And remember, it doesn't cost a thing to look!

The Paladion is located at 777 Front Street between F and G streets.

A few blocks away is the Gaslamp Quarter, where you can take a stroll into San Diego's past. Wyatt Earp once ran three gambling houses here, and sailors came looking for a good time after long months at sea. The Gaslamp was the city's notorious red light district, known as the "Stingaree." Historians say the name probably came from the stingray in San Diego Bay. But it was said you could be stung just as badly in the bordellos and bars of the Stingaree.

Business boomed. In the late 1880s, the Stingaree had about 70 saloons, with names such as "Old Tub of Blood" and "First and Last Chance Saloon," and 120 bordellos. Among the hundreds of call girls who made a living here was a feisty redhead, Ida Bailey. In 1903, "Madame" Bailey

Horton Plaza

opened her own brothel in a pale yellow house with a white picket fence. Here she and her girls entertained the city's rich and famous, including the mayor and police chief.

In the mid-1970s, merchants and property owners started a movement to save and restore the Gaslamp's Victorian architecture. In 1980, the sixteen-and-a-half-block area was designated a National Historic District.

Stroll through the Gaslamp today, and you'll see fine examples of Victorian-style commercial buildings built between the Civil War and World War I, as well as Oriental-style architecture in the city's Chinatown. Chinese immigrants settled here in the late 1800s, working as fishermen, farmers, storekeepers, and railroad workers, adding to the city's rich cultural heritage.

Today, little of the Gaslamp's bawdy past remains. Most of the peep shows, topless bars and X-rated bookstores have been replaced with trendy bistros and boutiques. There's a vibrant night life, with many new restaurants, clubs, and coffee houses. The Italian restaurants, Fio's and Sfuzzi's, on Fifth Avenue are usually jammed. And across the street from Fio's, Croce's Bar provides cool jazz on hot summer nights. The owner is Ingrid Croce, widow of the late singer Jim Croce. Their son A. J. often plays here. Also on Fifth is Ole Madrid, a Spanish restaurant with a disco in the basement.

Among the hotels here is the Horton Grand, now more than one hundred years old, restored to its turn-of-the-century charm. The bellhops even wear knickers. Guest rooms have gas fireplaces and period furniture, antique armoires and headboards. Some, legend has it, are inhabited by ghosts. One ghost, the story goes, was a gambler in the 1880s, shot in the back by his partner and stuffed in an armoire. It's said he's still hanging around the Horton Grand after all these years, trying to figure out why his partner would cross him. (Either that, or he likes room service.)

The Gaslamp Quarter is bordered by Broadway and L Street, between Fourth and Sixth avenues.

Coronado

From downtown, take the ferry, or drive the long blue curve of bridge over to Coronado Island. To the right, you can catch a breathtaking view of the San Diego skyline, and a covey of boats

(Opposite) Sailing in San Diego Bay

gently rocking in the bay. Coronado is an old community that seems a throwback to a simpler time. There are elegant, turn-of-the-century mansions here, along with neat rows of houses from the 1940s and '50s. On Coronado's Main Street, Orange Avenue, you can spread your blanket by the gazebo, and listen to a summer concert. Some of San Diego's oldest families live here, along with newer Navy families. Many were so captivated with Coronado during tours here that they returned to retire.

Coronado is rich in naval history. It was here that naval aviation was born. And the Naval Air Station North Island, on the tip of the peninsula, is still one of the most important air and sea complexes on the West Coast. During World War II, it was a vital training, staging, and development center for ships and air squadrons.

Charles Lindbergh flew the *Spirit of St. Louis* from North Island on May 10, 1927, on the first leg of his history-making transatlantic flight. The plane was built on North Island, financed by businessmen from St. Louis.

But perhaps Coronado is best known for the Hotel del Coronado—"The Del" to locals. This grand old Victorian, with its red towers and turrets, has been a local landmark for more than a hundred years. Twelve presidents have slept here, the movie *Some Like It Hot* was filmed here, and generations of tourists have flocked to its broad sweep of beach.

The Del was built at a time when President Grover Cleveland ran the White House, and Wyatt Earp ran Tombstone. Railroad tycoon Elisha Babcock and his partner, piano magnate H. L. Story, wanted to build a resort hotel that would be the "talk of the Western World."

The Del opened on February 19, 1888. At a cost of more than a million dollars, it was the most expensive hotel built on the West Coast. And it was the largest structure, outside of New York City, to have electric lights. Thomas Edison himself supervised the installation. This was such new-fangled stuff that each guest room had a card which read: "This room is equipped with the Edison Electric Light. Do not attempt to light with a match. Simply turn key on the wall by the door. The use of electricity for lighting is in no way harmful to health, nor does it affect soundness of sleep."

Over the years, this National Historic Landmark has been visited by the famous and infamous. It was the site of a dinner honoring Charles Lindbergh after his transatlantic flight. And it was here that the Prince of Wales is said to have met Wallis Simpson for the first time in 1920 at a state dinner. She was then the wife of the commanding officer of nearby North Island Naval Air Station. Sixteen years later, King Edward VII gave up his throne to marry "the woman I love."

You don't have to be a royal to dine in the Del's main dining salon, the Crown Room, but you'll feel like one. This majestic room has a curved pine ceiling that soars thirty feet high. (You feel as if you've been swallowed up in the bowels of a great whale.) It is something of an engineering marvel; there are no nails or interior supports. It's held together solely with wooden pegs. Four lighted crowns are suspended from the ceiling. The Crown Room may be expensive, but it doesn't cost a king's ransom.

You can also dine in the intimate Prince of Wales Restaurant or outside on the Ocean Terrace with its red-and-white umbrellas overlooking the beach and tennis courts. In the lobby's Palm Court, you can sink into a Victorian-style chair, order a drink or coffee, and watch the world pass by. At Christmas time, the lobby lights up with a magnificent Christmas tree soaring several stories high. Thomas Edison is said to have pulled the switch on the Del's first electrically-illuminated Christmas tree.

Over the generations, the white-and-red gazebo in the garden has been the setting for countless weddings. It is one of the many special places here that gives the Del a sense of history.

So pull up a wicker chair, or stroll the paths along the beach. And drink in the sweet scent of jasmine and geraniums. This is the place to loll your days away, at the grand old lady by the sea.

Head south out of the Del onto Silver Strand Boulevard (it becomes 75), and you'll soon come to the Loews Coronado Bay Resort, as new as the Del is old. It's on a private peninsula surrounded by water, and has its own eighty-slip marina where you can rent sailboats and wave runners or catch a shoppers' water taxi service to Coronado and San Diego Harbor. RRR's Cafe overlooks the colorful marina, offering dining inside and al fresco. (The name comes from a nautical term that means "red right returning," directing sailors to observe the right of way down a channel.) The restaurant has an airy feeling, filled with natural wood and wicker. There's also a market and deli, where they'll pack a custom picnic for beach or boat. In the more formal Azzura Point Restaurant upstairs, you can watch the lights of San Diego dance across the bay while you dine. The seafood is excellent here. The restaurant is washed in white with wicker chairs and striped canvas cushions, a cool, comfortable spot.

On the other side of Coronado, Le Meridien covers sixteen acres along the waterfront near the foot of the Coronado Bridge. Here you'll find breathtaking views of San Diego Bay and the city skyline. The resort is known for luxury. There are three hundred rooms and suites, and a village of villas with their own pool.

Marius is the resort's award-winning restaurant, serving Provencal cuisine in elegant rooms

The Gaslamp Quarter

The Paladion

hung with still lifes of fruit and vegetables. L'Escale offers dining outside under green umbrellas, with green-and-white-striped canvas chairs, and a view of the pool and bay beyond. Or have a drink in the clubby La Provence.

Le Meridien Spa and Clarins Institut de Beaute will pamper and polish you. It offers a range of skin care, massage, and stress-reducing treatments, along with a personal fitness profile and program to get you in shape. There are fitness facilities, along with three pools and six lighted "deco-turf" tennis courts, two whirlpools, and an eighteen-hole golf course across the street. There's also jet skiing, sailing, deep sea fishing. Or you can bike or stroll along the broad paths overlooking the bay.

Not far away is the Old Ferry Landing with dozens of shops and cafes and Peohe's Restaurant, consistently rated the best dining with a view.

The ferry departs from the Broadway Pier off Harbor Drive in San Diego every hour on the hour from 7:00 a.m. to 10:00 p.m. (11:00 p.m. on Friday and Saturday) seven days a week all year round.

Point Loma / Cabrillo National Monument

It's a long trek to the tip of Point Loma and the Cabrillo National Monument. But the vista—a spectacular 360-degree view of San Diego Harbor, the ocean, and the mountains—is well worth the drive. It's a perfect place to watch Navy ships sailing into the harbor or planes taking off from the Naval Air Station North Island. You might even see gray whales on their annual migration if you visit between late December and late February. Every year, they pass Point Loma on the way from the Arctic Ocean to Baja California, a journey of five thousand miles. The park also offers exhibits, tours, and films.

The site commemorates Juan Rodriquez Cabrillo, the Portuguese explorer who discovered what is now California on September 28, 1542. Fifty years after Columbus arrived in the New World, Cabrillo set out on his voyage of discovery from the Mexican port of Navidad. He had a commission to find a sea route to the Atlantic Ocean, around what was then believed to be the island of California. His patron, the Viceroy of Mexico, Antonio de Mendoza, was motivated by the glitter of gold. Legend had it that Califia was the fictional queen of an island kingdom where Amazon warriors carried swords of gold because there was no other metal on the island.

Cabrillo did not find gold, but what he did find was ultimately far more valuable: eight hundred miles of coastline in what would be known as the Golden State. His expedition explored the length of the coast, from Baja to what is now Oregon. And he saw the islands now called Santa Catalina, San Clemente, and San Miguel.

But Cabrillo's quest would kill him. He broke his leg and died from complications six weeks later. A statue of Cabrillo now looks out over the ocean he sailed, the coast he discovered.

While you're here, take a look at the Old Point Loma Lighthouse. A keeper climbed the winding stairs and lit an oil lamp here for the first time on November 15, 1855. For thirty-six years, the lighthouse guided sailors into San Diego Harbor. But fog and clouds often shrouded the light. So on March 23, 1891, the keeper put out the flame for the last time. Today you can visit the refurbished lighthouse which stands as a sentinel to San Diego's sailing past.

The San Diego Zoo

The San Diego Zoo started out with a scattering of specimens, left after the close of the 1915-1916 Panama-California International Exposition. The zoo has grown to one of the world's biggest and best—a one hundred-acre tropical garden with four thousand animals, representing eight hundred species. Most live in barless enclosures that look, and even sound, like their natural homes in the wild.

The Gorilla Tropics, for instance, has the best stereo system in town. Lowland gorillas hear the primitive sounds of a rain forest, recorded on location in Africa. Compact discs play the sounds on dozens of speakers hidden throughout the tropics. The exhibit covers two-and-a-half acres, filled with waterfalls, pools, and plants. There's even a cavernous free flight aviary, with hundreds of exotic African birds. You'll go ape over it all.

Tiger River takes you on a trip through a three-acre Asian rain forest. You'll see hundreds of mammals, reptiles, and birds, including Chinese water dragons, Malayan tapirs, and Sumatran

The Immaculata, University of San Diego

24

Library, U. C. San Diego

County Administration Center

tigers. Besides the fauna, there's a half million dollars worth of exotic flowers and plants. Here, Mother Nature gets a little help from high technology—a computer-controlled fogging system creates mist and humidity not normally found in San Diego's dry climate.

The Sun Bear Forest is like a big playpen for these mischievous Malayan bears, tree dwellers from Southeast Asia and Borneo. The bears "trashed" their multi-million dollar enclosure. So the zoo had to build another one, but this time it's "bear-proof." These comical bears are real crowd pleasers: they sure know how to clown around!

And don't forget the colony of koalas, the most popular critters in the zoo. In fact, these cuddly creatures have become synonymous with the San Diego Zoo, the first zoo in the United States to exhibit them.

Kids of all ages will love the Children's Zoo, with its "petting paddock," walk-through bird cages, incubator, and nursery where baby animals are bottle-fed and diapered.

You can see the zoo by bus on a forty-minute tour, or by air, 170 feet up, on the Skyfari aerial tram. Hungry? There's plenty of feeding time for both animals and humans (from hot dogs and sodas to finer fare).

The zoo is open from 9:00 a.m. daily year round. Gates generally close at 4:00 or 5:00 p.m., depending on the season. It's located on Zoo Drive, in Balboa Park.

Balboa Park

Balboa Park is the largest in the country, lush grounds and botanical gardens stretching for 1,400 acres. It's a delightful place to spread your blanket and while away a summer's day, explore the many museums, or meander along the walkways. There's a bit of magic at every turn. Actors performing Shakespeare in a garden grotto. Children splashing in a fountain. Spanish music drifting through the trees. The park's one hundred-bell carillon tolls hour after hour. Even so, there's a sense of timelessness here.

The beautiful old Spanish-Moorish buildings were constructed for the Panama-California International Exposition of 1915-1916, to celebrate the opening of the Panama Canal. They were intended as temporary structures, but, luckily, the city fathers made the buildings a permanent part of the park. And later construction followed the original Spanish theme.

Stroll El Prado, the park's "main street," lined with museums. Here you'll also find native dancers and musicians, palm readers and painters. (Christmas on the Prado has become a San Diego tradition. Museums are free, and there's festive food and entertainment.)

Just past the lily pond, sometimes teaming with tadpoles, is the Botanical Building, a grand wooden "birdcage" filled with exotic plants. Continue down El Prado to the plaza where you'll find the San Diego Museum of Art, and the House of Hospitality (there's an information office here).

Hang a left and head for the Organ Pavilion. Here, on January 1, 1915, sugar magnates John D. and Adolph Spreckels presented the city with a colossal gift: what's considered to be the world's largest outdoor musical instrument. The Spreckels pipe organ can be heard two miles away at times. It takes a twenty-horsepower electric blower to provide the huge volume of air to operate the organ. And what a set of pipes—4,416 to be exact. You can get a sample every Sunday afternoon at two during free public concerts.

If you make a right at the Organ Pavilion, you'll see the Hall of Nations and the House of Pacific Relations, a cluster of cottages devoted to the cultures of different nations: China, Czechoslovakia, Germany, Hungary, Ireland, Israel, Norway, and others. The cottages are open on weekends, and on national holidays celebrations are often held in the center courtyard.

Among the many museums in the park: The Reuben H. Fleet Space Theater and Science Center, featuring large-format Omnimax films; San Diego Museum of Art, with a permanent collection rich in Indian and Asian art, masterpieces by El Greco, Goya, Matisse, O'Keefe, Toulouse-Lautrec, and cutting-edge California artists; the San Diego Natural History Museum with exhibits on minerals, the sea, shore, and desert, and California's endangered species; the San Diego Aerospace Museum and International Aerospace Hall of Fame, tracing flight from its birth through the space age, with exhibits on aviation heroes, even a moon rock.

If all that museum-hopping makes you hungry, grab a light lunch at the Sculpture Garden Cafe by the San Diego Museum of Art or at the Cafe del Rey Moro in the House of Hospitality.

For entertainment, the Simon Edison Centre for the Performing Arts includes the Lowell Davies Festival Theatre, the Cassius Carter Centre Stage, and the Old Globe Theatre, which offers both classic and contemporary works, as well as the summer Shakespeare Festival. The Starlight Bowl presents summer musicals in its outdoor amphitheatre. And the Casa del Prado Theatre hosts the Junior Theatre, Youth Symphony, and the San Diego Gilbert and Sullivan Company.

Coronado Ferry

(Opposite) Hotel Del Coronado

Old Town

Old Town is San Diego's birthplace. It was little more than a collection of ramshackle buildings and adobe houses when the city was incorporated in 1850. But the area's colorful history begins long before that.

The first San Diegans were Indians, now called Tipai and Ipai, meaning "people" by anthropologists. The Spaniards who came later called the Indians "San Dieguenos," and set about trying to Christianize them.

On July 16, 1769, Father Junipero Serra founded the first California Mission, called San Diego de Alcala, on Presidio Hill overlooking what is now Old Town. That site did not have adequate water, so the mission was later moved to its present location along the San Diego River. Most of the original structures were destroyed by a fire and two earthquakes, but Father Serra's living quarters and the church facade survived. You can visit the rebuilt mission, and the museum, chapel, and gardens at 10818 San Diego Mission Road in Mission Valley.

For fifty years, San Diego's life centered on the mission and presidio, or fort. But gradually, soldiers and other settlers moved down the hill to Old Town, to cultivate plots of land. A plaza was laid out here in the early 1820s, as the center of this new settlement. Over the next fifteen years, the town grew steadily. In the mid-1830s, Richard Henry Dana Jr. described Old Town as "about forty dark brown looking huts ... and three or four larger ones, white-washed, which belonged to the 'gente de razon,'" that is, the upper class. As the settlement grew, the Presidio declined and was eventually abandoned.

Over the years, the area changed hands: in 1821, when Mexico won its independence from Spain, and again, in 1846, when the United States laid claim to California during its war with Mexico. A treaty signed in 1848 put California, Texas, and New Mexico under U.S. control.

Old Town grew for a time under the Americans. But gradually, Alonzo Horton's New Town near the wharf attracted commerce, and became the center of San Diego. To make matters worse, a fire in 1872 destroyed many of Old Town's buildings.

Today, you can still get a glimpse into the city's past, along six square blocks of historic buildings, shops, and restaurants.

Stop at the Whaley House on San Diego Avenue, built in 1856, Southern California's first two-story brick building. Though modest by today's standards, it was considered a mansion back then.

It was built by businessman Thomas Whaley, whose spirit is said to make appearances now and then. Just ask June Reading, director of the Whaley House, and she'll give you an earful. "This house is alive," she says, "with noises and sounds and fragrances." Reading claims she, herself, has seen Whaley: "a short man in a black frock coat, black pantaloons, and a broad-brimmed hat." And at times, the odor of his favorite Havana cigars wafts through the main hall.

It's said his wife, Anna, has also been sighted. Witnesses swear they've smelled her heavy, sweet perfume, or heard the rustle of her skirts on the stairs. Even the family's pet terrier, Dolly Varden, has been seen running through the house, only to disappear. Or at least, that's what they say.

If that's not enough spirits for one house, Yankee Jim Robinson is reported to walk the floor upstairs. He was hanged in 1852 on the spot where Whaley later built his house. It was a stiff sentence for trying to steal a schooner worth $6,500. And until the moment he died, Yankee Jim thought the authorities were just trying to scare him, not hang him. He was dead wrong. And he must have died with his boots on. Reading says footsteps on the second floor sound like "a big man wearing boots."

Whether you believe that or not, the Whaley House is listed as one of thirty ghost houses by the U.S. Department of Commerce. It's one of only two in California.

In addition to being the home of the Whaley family, the house served as a granary, country store, church, courthouse, public school, and the town's first theatre.

Today, you can tour the courtroom and parlor on the first floor, and bedrooms on the second, furnished with antiques. And maybe you'll even see Thomas Whaley if you're lucky.

Down the street from the Whaley House is the Old Town State Historic Park, a collection of restored and reconstructed buildings which recreate California life from 1821 to 1872. Walking tours begin every day at 2:00 p.m. at the Robinson-Rose Building, now the visitor center. You can explore adobe houses, haciendas, a blacksmith's shop, and a restored newspaper office where the first edition of the *San Diego Union* came off the press in 1868.

Another point of historical interest is La Casa de Estudillo, an adobe house considered one of the finest remnants of Mexican California. A retired presidio commandante began construction in 1827, but died before it was completed. His son continued the work. Rooms are laid out around a central courtyard, including La Sala or family room, a study, bedrooms, and a chapel. Food

"Here's looking at you"

A koala at the San Diego Zoo

was prepared outside in the kitchen area under a veranda. Rooms have beamed ceilings, whitewashed walls, and brick floors. Furnishings include original pieces from the Mexican and Early American periods, as well as reproductions.

The Mason Street School House, built in 1865, was San Diego's first school. The first teacher, Mary Chase Walker, made sixty-five dollars a month. She retired after less than a year to marry the head of the school board. More than a hundred years later, this one-room schoolhouse is still used for education—adult classes in California history are taught there.

Seeley Stable is a reconstructed stable and barns, housing a collection of horse-drawn vehicles, western memorabilia, and Indian artifacts, some thousands of years old. In 1867, Albert Seeley started the San Diego-Los Angeles Stage Line. His stagecoaches made the 130-mile trip in less than twenty-four hours, a trip that now takes about three.

La Casa de Bandini, a beautiful hacienda built in 1829 for Juan Bandini, was a social center during Mexican rule. It was later sold to Albert Seeley, who added a second floor and opened the Cosmopolitan Hotel. Now it houses a popular restaurant. The central courtyard is framed by citrus trees, birds of paradise, and palms. Sit outside under green-striped umbrellas, and listen to strolling mariachis while you sip a margarita.

And don't miss Bazaar del Mundo, a colorful collection of shops and restaurants laid out around a courtyard, abloom with plants and flowers. On weekends, Spanish and Mexican dancers add to the festive atmosphere. And many of the shops sell Mexican folk arts and crafts. There are several restaurants to choose from, including Casa de Pico, where you can have a fiesta along with your feast.

The bazaar is located near the plaza at Juan and Wallace streets.

Other restaurants in Old Town are Cafe Pacifica, consistently rated one of the finest for fish, and the Old Town Mexican Cafe, where you can watch tortillas being made while you wait for a table. Both are on San Diego Avenue.

Next door to the cafe is the Old Town Esplanade, a two-level shopping complex where stores sell everything from stuffed bears to Birkenstock sandals. There's also the Coyote Cafe and the open-air Coyote Cactus Bar.

Climb up Harney Street to Heritage Park, and its collection of restored Victorian homes from the late 1800s. They now house offices, antique shops, and the Heritage Park Bed & Breakfast Inn.

Seaport Village horse-drawn carriage

Old Point Loma lighthouse

Mission San Diego de Alcala

To complete your tour, take a winding road up to Presidio Park, overlooking Old Town. The original buildings no longer exist, but tiles from the Presidio chapel were salvaged, and used to fashion a twenty-eight foot cross on the site. At the Junipero Serra Museum and Library, exhibits trace the adventures of Indians, Spanish explorers and priests, and the first Mexican and American settlers. This forty-acre park is also a favorite with picnickers . . . and lovers . . . who sit on its grassy slopes and watch the city bustle below them—a city that was born in Old Town.

To reach Old Town, take the Old Town Avenue exit off Interstate 5, and turn left on San Diego Avenue.

Sea World

Sea World is a 150-acre marine park, the most visited of all San Diego attractions, offering shows, exhibits, aquariums and rides.

Its most famous finny creature is Shamu, the killer whale. But Shamu has lots of friends—Baby Shamu, Namu, Nakina, and Splash (the only male). The whales perform to delighted crowds in Shamu Stadium. Sit in the first twelve rows, and you're sure to get wet! Shamu Vision, a three hundred-square foot TV screen, gives you a good view no matter where you sit.

There are also dolphins, sea lions and otters, walruses, exotic marine birds, sea turtles, and sharks! The Shark Encounter has the world's largest display of sharks—more than eighty of them glide in 680,000 gallons of saltwater.

Other features include the Penguin Encounter, with more than three hundred Antarctic penguins in a frosty environment; Forbidden Reef, where you can feed bat rays in a shallow lagoon and come face to face with moray eels; and always a favorite, the sea lion and otter show.

Feed the fish, or feed your face at the many fast food restaurants and snack bars.

You can take a six-minute skyride over Mission Bay, or see all of Sea World and San Diego on the Skytower, a 320-foot spiral into the sky. If you want to keep your feet on the ground, go for the ninety-minute walking tour with expert guides.

Sea World opens daily at 9:00 a.m. Closing time depends on the season.
To reach the park, exit west from Interstate 5 onto Sea World Drive.

Mission Bay / Mission Beach

Not far away is Mission Bay Park, a favorite recreation spot for families. Here the waters are sheltered and shallow for swimming. Sailing and windsurfing are also popular. There are grassy places for family picnics, playgrounds for kids, and miles of sidewalks for strolling. And on breezy afternoons, kite-flyers will dazzle with their aerial acrobatics. Mission Bay Park is off Mission Boulevard, West Mission Bay Drive, and Ingraham Street.

Perhaps San Diego's most visited beach is Mission Beach, a sort of human carnival on the sand. The boardwalk here has been compared to a Fellini movie: colorful, sometimes bizarre people abound. There's South Mission Beach where San Diego State students major in volleyball. And there's North Mission where my colleague, Larry Himmel, says, "you're never too old to surf, or too young to skateboard." I agree with Larry that Mission Beach "is more than just a place, it's an attitude."

There's also Belmont Park, a beachfront amusement and shopping center, where you can ride the Giant Dipper roller coaster (top speeds of 40 to 45 mph) and the Liberty Carousel, or dive into the Plunge, the largest indoor pool in southern California.

To reach Mission Beach, exit I-5 at Garnet Avenue and head west to Mission Boulevard.

La Jolla

La Jolla means "the jewel" in Spanish, and for residents and visitors alike, this seaside town is a gem. A century ago, it attracted a colony of artists who tried to capture its rocky shores and special light. Today, it's a wealthy community, where property values have soared, a posh playground for well-heeled townspeople and tourists. Even though La Jolla has a cosmopolitan feel, the city fathers (and mothers) have tried hard to retain its village character and charm.

Stroll along palm-lined Prospect, browse in the toney boutiques and art galleries, or dine al fresco at the many restaurants here. George's at the Cove and Top of the Cove are favorites for not only the food, but the view. The locals gather at Pannikin for steaming cups of coffee,

Museum of Man, Balboa Park

Museum of Man and gardens

scones, and croissants. And at the Hard Rock Cafe, filled with rock music memorabilia, the waitresses are straight out of central casting. They serve up a lot of ham with the burgers. For a little culture, it's a short walk to the Museum of Contemporary Art, San Diego, with its permanent collection of post-1950 art.

The centerpiece of town is the wonderful old Spanish-style La Valencia Hotel, with its pink stucco and bougainvillaea. As you enter, you'll pass beneath the colonnade with a palm-shaded Tropical Patio to your left. The lobby is Spanish tile, with a huge bouquet of flowers on the marble-topped table. Off the lobby, an elegant drawing room has a floor-to-ceiling window overlooking La Jolla Cove. Sink into a comfortable chair and drink in the view, or have a drink outside on the terrace.

There's also the dark and cozy Whaling Bar & Grill, a popular watering hole. The bar has a collection of New Bedford harpoons, scrimshaw, model ships, and murals by Wing Howard. Take the elevator to the sky—the Sky Room Restaurant, that is. It offers the loftiest view of the La Jolla shoreline. This plush little place has only a dozen tables, a prix fixe menu, and a dazzling 180-degree view of the Pacific. You can also dine outside on the patio, or in the adjoining Mediterranean Room with ocean view.

La Valencia opened on December 15, 1926, soon attracting the wealthy and celebrated. In those days, a room cost as much as ten dollars a day. Sounds like a bargain now, but back then, it was a week's pay. During the 1930s, La Valencia was the perfect hideaway for Hollywood stars: Charlie Chaplin, Greta Garbo, Lillian Gish, Groucho Marx, Mary Pickford, the Talmadge sisters.

When the La Jolla Playhouse was founded in 1947, the Valencia became the gathering place for a new generation of stars: playhouse founders Gregory Peck, Dorothy McGuire, and Mel Ferrer, along with Ginger Rogers, Jennifer Jones, and David Niven, to name just a few. Peck was artistic director for a time. And on opening nights, he hosted cast parties in the Whaling Bar.

Over the years, the Valencia has had a loyal following. It's a gathering place for San Diegans as well as visitors. Many weddings and other special occasions, marking time and tradition, have been celebrated here.

Perhaps a puzzle explains La Valencia's appeal. Almost since the day the hotel opened, there's been a jigsaw puzzle on the table in the lounge. Guests have studied it, been stumped by it. They've added pieces here and there. As Bruce Dexter writes in a pamphlet on the hotel,

"Every visitor to the hotel added a little something, left behind a little something of themselves, to help form the overall picture of Valencia." Today, guests are still adding pieces to the puzzle.

When you're finished exploring La Valencia, take a stroll around La Jolla Cove, with its lovely palm-lined park overlooking the surf, a sanctuary for fish and wildlife. You can watch the sea lions sun themselves on the rocks, or sun yourself on the beach. Swim and snorkel in the underwater preserve, one of the prime places in San Diego to see marine life. Farther south is Windansea Beach, a favorite of surfers, made famous in Tom Wolfe's *The Pumphouse Gang*, about teen-agers who staked out the sand there in the sixties.

The highest point in La Jolla is Mt. Soledad, site of a cross that's become a local landmark. From here you have a breathtaking view of the coast.

Take Torrey Pines Road out of town, and stop in at the Marine Room for dinner or a drink. It has arguably the best beachside view in town, the waves framed by a wall of windows. The restaurant turned into an aquarium in the eighties, when high winds and heavy surf smashed through the glass. (The daily catch that day was especially fresh.)

If you follow the scenic drive out of town, you can take a quick detour and pass through the beach-and-bedroom community of La Jolla Shores. There's a short main street with surf shops and other stores, and Piatti, a chic Italian restaurant. For a place to stay, there's the Sea Lodge, a couple of blocks down on the beach. On hot summer days it seems as if all of La Jolla flocks here, to bake on the sand, stroll the boardwalk, or picnic in the park.

Back on North Torrey Pines Road, stop in at the new Stephen Birch Aquarium-Museum on a bluff overlooking the ocean. This $14-million facility has a panoramic view of the Pacific, and a man-made tide pool.

The aquarium is to the right of the galleria, just past a tank filled with silvery sardines. There are thirty-three tanks in all (the biggest is fifty thousand gallons) filled with technicolored fish. Taking a tour through the aquarium is a little like taking a voyage with Scripps scientists. Here, you can explore the waters of the Pacific Northwest, Southern California, Mexico's Sea of Cortez, and the South Pacific. In one display, moon jelly fish look like white parachutes drifting through space. In another, pink and silver fish dart about in an aquatic ballet. You'll see brilliant orange garibaldi, a gigantic grouper, the flowery tentacles of the sand rose anemone, and rainbow-colored fish cavorting in a coral reef.

The centerpiece of the facility is the giant kelp forest, a seventy thousand-gallon tank (sixteen feet deep), filled with marine life from off the coast of La Jolla. Designers used underwater

Botanical building, Balboa Park

Statue of Spanish Conquistador, Balboa Park

photographs to come up with an exhibit that looks like the real thing. You can view it all through a thirteen-foot acrylic wall, weighing in at ten tons.

To the left of the galleria is the museum, with a permanent exhibition on oceanography, "Exploring the Blue Planet." Here you can learn about earthquakes, weather patterns, and ocean life. The museum has all manner of scientific exhibits, many of them hands-on, including a wave machine (where you can make your own) and the Ocean Supermarket, a sort of shoppers' guide to products from the sea. Using a scanner gun, you can "read" the bar codes on products you'd find in your local grocery. You learn that frosting and fudge sauce, for instance, contain seaweed. The display shows how our lives are closely linked to the sea.

The aquarium is part of the world famous Scripps Institution of Oceanography at the University of California, San Diego. It's located at 2300 Expedition Way.

Wind your way along North Torrey Pines Road, past the Salk Institute and the Torrey Pines Glider Port where hang-gliders take to the skies, soaring off sandstone cliffs overlooking the ocean. Continue on, and you'll pass the Scripps Clinic and Research Foundation, along with the Sheraton Grande Torrey Pines, the Torrey Pines Golf Course, and Torrey Pines State Reserve.

All take their name from the twisted *Pinus torreyana*, the rarest pine tree in the United States. It now grows only on this reserve and on Santa Rosa Island off the coast near Santa Barbara. The reserve also has a museum with exhibits of its natural and cultural history. In addition, a half-dozen hiking trails snake through the pines, offering spectacular views of the Pacific and other natural features—baroque sandstone formations, spring flowers and the famous Torrey Pines themselves.

Some of the trails lead to the very edge of the sandstone cliffs overlooking the ocean below. Another route takes you down to the beach on a narrow, precipitous trail. Take a stroll on the strand and look up at the cliffs, worn by wind and water and striped with bands of terra cotta, ochre, and verdigris. You can sun yourself on Flat Rock, or poke through the tide pools. Another quarter mile south is Black's Beach where swimsuits are definitely optional. Nudity is banned here, but that doesn't prevent sunbathers from baring, and braving, it all anyway. (Bring some extra sunscreen.)

To reach the trails and museum, you can drive up the hill, or park your car at the base, and hoof it. The rules are strict: no smoking, campfires, or picnics permitted. And forget the souvenirs. Leave plants, animals, and rocks behind for fellow travelers to enjoy.

Del Mar

From Torrey Pines State Reserve, it's a five-minute drive to the charming beach community of Del Mar (if you're on Interstate 5, get off at Del Mar Heights Road, and head west to the ocean). The town's main avenue, Camino Del Mar, is lined with boutiques, surf shops, real estate offices, and restaurants.

At the north end of town is Del Mar Plaza, a shopping and dining complex just blocks from the ocean. There you can settle into an Adirondack chair on the piazza overlooking the Pacific. It's beautifully landscaped with terra cotta pots abloom with flowers, pools, and fountains where sculptured "people" cool their heels on a hot summer's day. (They look so real, you'll do a double take.)

You can sip an Italian aperitif under an umbrella at the outdoor Enoteca ("wine library" in Italian), or belly up to the take-out bar and order mozzarella e pomodoro, a plate of olives and parmesan, and a good, crusty bread. You can also dine in, or out, at the many good restaurants here, all with ocean views: Fornaio for Italian, Epazote's for Mexican, Pacifica Del Mar for seafood with the taste of the Pacific Rim. The plaza also has fast-food vegetarian, fiftys diner fare, and a gelato parlor for dessert. Or you can pick up a picnic at Daniel's Market, choosing from pasta salads and pates. The Plaza also has men's and women's boutiques, art galleries, jewelry and gift shops, and a good book store.

Del Mar Plaza is located at 1555 Camino Del Mar.

Across the street is L'Auberge Del Mar, a small, elegant hotel (only 123 rooms) now affiliated with L.A.'s prestigious Bel Air Hotel. It's on the site overlooking the sea where the original Stratford Inn (later the Hotel Del Mar) was once the town's centerpiece, and a haven for Hollywood stars. In the 1920s, Douglas Fairbanks Sr. and Mary Pickford were frequent guests, along with Charlie Chaplin, tennis great Bill Tilden, Jack Dempsey, George Burns and Gracie Allen.

Jesse Shepherd House, "Villa Montezuma," 1887

Victorian houses at Heritage Park, Old Town

Serra Museum, Presidio Park

The present hotel borrows from the past. Off the lobby, the Jimmy Durante Pub was dedicated in honor of the unofficial mayor of Del Mar "in memory of many happy evenings around the piano at the original Hotel Del Mar." Durante used to have a beach house, and was a frequent visitor to the nearby Del Mar Race Track. Today, in the pub that bears his name, you can peruse old pictures of Durante and his wife, Marge, along with Eddie Cantor, Jack Benny, and other Hollywood stars. The pub has a massive, double-sided brick fireplace, a replica of one found in the old hotel. The library and music room is dedicated to Desi Arnaz, who shared a nearby beach home with Lucille Ball. The inn's restaurant, Tourlas, is named after the original chef of the old Hotel Del Mar, but offers up new California cuisine.

In the hotel lobby, sink into a comfortable couch or overstuffed chair and order tea and scones while you listen to music from the baby grand. French doors lead to a terrace overlooking a landscaped garden and pool, and the blue Pacific beyond.

Across from the hotel, at Fifteenth Street and Camino Del Mar, is Stratford Square, an English tudor-style structure that houses, among other businesses, Carlos and Annie's for burgers, and for a brew, J.J. McGuire's pub. It used to house the "Schwabs of Del Mar," a drug store and soda fountain where Hollywood stars used to hang out during racing season. Historians say it was "the" place to go, a sort of gossip central. It's said that Jennifer Jones ordered thick, syrupy sundaes topped with lots of whipped cream. Rita Hayworth liked vanilla; Bud Abbott, chocolate.

It's a short walk from Stratford Square down to the beach and the Del Mar train depot, where the locals can set their clocks by the Amtrak trains that run south to downtown San Diego, north to Los Angeles and beyond.

Del Mar Race Track

Del Mar has long been an escape for Angelenos in the summertime. Hollywood stars flocked here in the thirties and forties to bask on the beach and play the horses at the Del Mar Race Track. The track, as the song says, is "where the turf meets the surf." Crooner Bing Crosby not only sang the song, he founded the track in 1937. Crosby was a horse breeder in nearby Rancho Santa Fe. Another entertainer, Pat O'Brien, was his principal partner, and other Hollywood pals joined in, including Oliver "Babe" Hardy, said to be a big horse player.

Casa de Estudillo, Old Town State Historic Park

Orca and trainer at Sea World

Dolphin feeding, Sea World

Entrance to Mission Beach

Mission Beach

Roller coaster, Belmont Park

(Opposite) Aerial view of La Jolla

The cove at La Jolla

La Jolla office complex

"The Children's Pool," La Jolla

Torrey Pines State Reserve

Parasailing at Torrey Pines

Del Mar fair

The Plaza at night, Del Mar

Thoroughbred racing, Del Mar

(Opposite) Del Mar Race Track

But the track was almost side-tracked, the story goes, until Crosby and O'Brien borrowed on their life insurance policies, and ponied up $400,000. Opening day was July 3, 1937, a gala event that drew fifteen thousand spectators, and stars such as Barbara Stanwyck and Robert Taylor. Crosby and O'Brien personally greeted fans as they passed through the gate. Douglas Fairbanks Sr. and his new wife, Lady Ashley, helped Bing celebrate the victory of his horse, High Strike, in the very first race at Del Mar. Opening Day at Del Mar has been a tradition ever since. Women and men alike wear their most elegant (or outrageous) hats to watch the races from the members-only Turf Club. (But it's hard to say which is more fun, watching the horses or the people.) Others pack picnics and fill coolers, and spread their blankets in the infield (you can bring your own booze, but no glass).

Bing himself would probably be surprised at how this little track by the sea has grown. The *Daily Racing Form* calls it the number one track in America, based on the daily average handle—more than $7.8 million—and the daily average attendance—more than thirty-seven thousand.

The racing season is late July through mid-September each year.

Rancho Santa Fe

This is where the other half lives ... Rancho Santa Fe. You reach it along winding country roads lined with white fences, groves of willow and eucalyptus trees. You'll pass sprawling ranches, equestrian centers and stables. Children practice dressage on Saturday mornings, and polo is played here on Sunday afternoons at the Rancho Santa Fe Polo Club.

Rancho Santa Fe village is charming, with Spanish-style architecture, white stucco, and red-tiled roofs. There are some boutiques and antique stores for browsing. But the village is short on shops, long on real estate offices. It's easy to see why. The median price of homes here is more than a million dollars. That's median.

There are a few restaurants of note: Bolero, Delicias, and Mille Fleurs, recently named by *Food and Wine Magazine* as one of the top twenty-five restaurants in the country. The restaurant blends classic French dishes with California cuisine. Bertrand Hug is the amiable owner.

The restaurant credits nearby Chino's Farm for produce that's become nationally known. Other restaurants—Alice Water's Chez Panisse in Berkeley and Wolfgang Puck's Spago in Los

Angeles, to name just two—fly Chino's produce in. On Saturday morning, Chino's looks like a luxury car lot, as well-heeled (and well-fed) customers line up for perfect produce and herbs. You can even listen to classical music as you squeeze the tomatoes. Join the crowd, but get there early.

A few miles away is the Rancho Valencia Resort, a haven for the tennis power set, with eighteen courts, a renowned tennis clinic, and pros to polish your game. There's even a very proper croquet court if you're feeling genteel.

The resort is set on forty acres of beautifully manicured grounds. The architecture is reminiscent of early California haciendas. In the main building, a Mexican-tiled courtyard has a fountain, fireplace, and terra cotta pots filled with flowers. It leads to the reception area, restaurant, and terrace overlooking the tennis courts.

Stay in intimate casitas, with amenities such as wet bars and fireplaces. There are also pools and a health spa (try a massage to soothe that tennis elbow). And when you're all relaxed after a hard day's fun, dine in the lovely restaurant with its high, beamed ceiling, fireplace, and gourmet meals. You can also sit outside in the courtyard, weather permitting.

Rancho Valencia is located at 5921 Valencia Circle in Rancho Santa Fe.

Balloon Rides

Perhaps the best way to see the North County is by air. Hot air balloon, that is. At $125 to $140 per person, it's not cheap, but it will definitely lift your spirits. You'll feel like Dorothy in the *Wizard of Oz* when you step into the basket. And once aloft, floating high above town and country, you'll know you aren't in Kansas anymore. Up here, the peace and quiet are broken only by the chatter of birds, and a gentle SWOOOSSHHH as hot air fills the balloon. Far from the bustling freeways and madding crowds, you get a sense of solitude and serenity. The landing can be a bit bumpy, but then, this is no MD-11. You're picked up by spotters who follow your flight path from the ground. Back on earth, your balloon pilot will toast you with champagne and hors d'oeuvres, and commemorate your flight with a certificate and pin. (It's pretty hokey, but fun.) The one-hour flights are at sunrise and sunset. But the entire experience takes about three and a half hours, including check-in, travel to the launch site in a van, inflation, and pick up. The baskets hold four

Rancho Santa Fe Polo Club

Hot Air Balloon Festival, Del Mar

to seven passengers, so unless you've got a big family, you'll be sharing the gondola with strangers. But you won't be strangers for long. There's something about getting crammed together in a balloon that makes people bond.

San Diego Wild Animal Park

The San Diego Wild Animal Park is a sprawling 2,200-acre sanctuary where animals roam free in settings designed to recreate their native homelands. Here you'll find 3,000 mammals and birds from 450 species.

The best way to see it all is by the Wgasa Bush Line Monorail, a fifty-minute safari-by-rail. Guides describe the animals you see, as well as their habitats—African and Asian plains and prairies carved from the mesas and canyons. On one trip during the spring, we saw baby animals just after birth, their mothers shielding them protectively as we passed.

If you don't want to take the train, there's a walking safari along the one and three-quarter-mile Kilimanjaro hiking trail. Here you can see tigers, cheetahs, and elephants, among others. Or you can go on a photo safari, if you book ahead. An open-air truck will take you into the heart of the preserve, giving you a look that's up close and personal. You can feed carrots to the giraffes; the rhinos prefer apples.

Nairobi Village recreates an African village with animals, exhibits, and a shopping bazaar. It includes Lemur Island and Gorilla Grotto. And kids go wild in the Petting Kraal, where gentle gazelle, antelope, and deer pose patiently for pictures.

The park has a number of animal shows, including free-flying birds. They'll amaze you not only with their aerial agility, but with their singing ability. Pancho the parrot has "I Left My Heart in San Francisco" down pat.

And there's plenty of flora . . . three million plants representing 3,200 species . . . in the park's exotic gardens. See the Australian Rain Forest, Fuchsia House, Baja California Garden, Conifer Arboretum, Bonsai Pavilion, and many others.

The Wild Animal Park is open from 9:00 a.m. daily until dusk. It's about thirty miles north of downtown via Interstate 15/ Highway 163.

Day Trips

Julian

Within an hour or two of San Diego, you can find the mountains, the desert, and the rolling hills of wine country.

The folks who live in the rustic mountain town of Julian call it simply "the Mountain." And a visit here is like stepping back in time. Many of the buildings which line Main Street date back to the early 1900s. You can still get a malt at the old-fashioned marble-topped soda fountain. And there's even a country store.

Julian used to be a gold rush town. Now the rush is for apples. Every fall, hordes of "lowlanders" throng this tiny town (population: 1,320) during the Julian Apple Days festival. They poke around the shops and line up for thick pieces of apple pie. It's estimated that about one hundred thousand apple pies are sold here in October alone.

For tourists from Southern California, Julian is about as close as they can come to a real change of season. They come for a slice of autumn as well as a piece of apple pie. Winter is another popular time when San Diegans flock here for something in short supply back home: snow!

To reach Julian, take Highway 78 East from Escondido, through Ramona, and the town of Santa Ysabel. Don't forget to stop at the family-run Dudley's Bakery for the house specialty, raisin date nut bread, hot from the oven. There are seventeen breads to choose from, including cheddar cheese and jalapeno. And at Manzanita Ranch, you can pick up fruit, cider, and pumpkins to bring home.

Temecula

The wine country of Temecula is about an hour's drive from San Diego along I-15 North, past rocky mountains, and rows of citrus and avocado groves. Exit at Rancho California Road, and head east. At first, you'll pass so many spanking new developments, you'll wonder how there could be room for wineries. But just four miles from the I-15 exit, you'll see row upon row of grapes stepped on the hillside about as far as the eye can see.

Bengal tiger, San Diego Wild Animal Park

(Opposite) Quail Botanical Gardens, Encinitas

This area was discovered in the 1840s by wine great Jean Louis Vignes, and rediscovered in the 1960s by growers and wine experts. It is a choice site for wine-growing, with a climate similar to the fine wine regions of southern France. Cool breezes from the Pacific flow through a gap in the coastal mountain range into the Temecula Valley. That creates the longer growing season needed for premium varietal grapes.

Stop first at the Culbertson Winery, with its Mediterranean-style manor house, for tours and tasting. Here you can learn how sparkling wine is produced, a method pioneered by French monk Dom Perignon three hundred years ago.

If all that tasting makes you hungry, Cafe Champagne provides indoor dining in a charming setting with flower-printed wallpaper and dried flowers. Or sit outside on the terrace cooled by ceiling fans, a fountain splashing nearby. At the Champagne Bar, a jukebox belts out big band sounds. There's also a gift shop and herb garden, where cafe chefs select fresh herbs to accent the daily specials.

The Culbertson Winery is located at 32575 Rancho California Road.

There are ten other wineries in the valley, ranging from large operations to small, family-run establishments. Many offer tours, tastings, and picnic tables overlooking the vineyards. All you need is a bottle of wine, a loaf of bread, and thou (don't forget the cheese).

If you want to make a weekend of it, there are a half dozen hostelries, including the Temecula Creek Inn with eighty-four rooms and a twenty-seven-hole championship golf course in a rustic setting. Dine or drink at the inn's Hemet Grill, decorated in tones of taupe, slate ,and sandstone, with Indian artifacts framed on the walls. The inn is at 44501 Rainbow Canyon Road. (Take the Indio/Highway 79 exit off I-15.)

Before you leave the valley, visit Old Town Temecula, preserved in the architectural style of the 1890s, with its gift and antique shops, museum and visitor's center, and restaurants. And for a bird's-eye view, take a balloon flight over the wine country.

Anza-Borrego Desert State Park

To reach this huge state reserve, drive east from Julian on route 78 for an hour or so and head north on S-3 until you reach the little town of Borrego Springs. The scenery will justify the long drive, especially in the springtime. Anyone who thinks the desert is dry and colorless hasn't been to Anza-Borrego in this season. For a few weeks each year, usually in April, the normally abstemious plants that blanket East County's hills and mesas blossom forth suddenly in a spendthrift display of color, a riot of oranges, reds, and yellows.

When Anza-Borrego is in bloom, thousands of pilgrims arrive to witness this rite of spring. In fact, on weekends the desert can get downright congested with cars and tour buses. So if you have a choice, visit the park during the week. But in any case don't miss it.

From Borrego Springs, follow the signs to Anza-Borrego itself. A good place to start your tour is the visitor's center which has a museum and garden where you can take a crash course in the ecology of the desert landscape.

Not far from the center are walking trails that should satisfy all but the most ambitious hikers. One of the most popular, the Palm Canyon Trail, follows a clear, spring-fed stream that winds out of the mountains to water the desert below. As you walk onward (and upward) you'll experience a remarkably varied terrain filled with flowering ocotillo, agave, and a host of other desert plants and cacti. Keep a sharp eye out and you may even catch a glimpse of the bighorn sheep that range in these parts.

A few miles up the trail is Palm Canyon, one of the last refuges for California's only native palm tree. This pleasant little oasis offers shady relief from the rigors of the trail. Here hikers can picnic beneath the trees, cool themselves in a waterfall that spills out of the rocks, or simply relax in preparation for the return trek.

Tijuana / Baja California

Just a half hour from downtown San Diego lies *La Línea*, the border between the United States and Mexico, the busiest crossing in the world. Drive across the border at San Ysidro, and spend a day browsing in Tijuana. Or head for the beaches of Baja, along a scenic coastal road.

Mission San Luis Rey, Oceanside

Desert flowers, Anza-Borrego Desert State Park

But unless you relish a one-to-two hour wait at the border on your return, *walk* . . . don't drive. You can leave your car in San Diego and take the San Diego Trolley from Kettner and C streets, or you can leave your car at the many lots off Interstate 805 just before the border. (One is located next to the San Diego Factory Outlet Center, where you can find great buys on merchandise from Mikasa, Izod / Gant, Bass Shoes, Levi's, Maidenform, Nike, and many other manufacturers.) From there, it's a short walk into Tijuana, or a quick shuttle ride. Head for Avenida Revolucion, perhaps the best place to see (and taste) Tijuana. Here you'll find eight blocks of restaurants, nightspots, and shops filled with Mexican arts and crafts, and leather goods. The Fronton Palacio, between Seventh and Eighth streets, offers a look at the world's fastest game, jai alai, and you can wager, too.

If you take a taxi or car, drive to the *Zona del Rio* (River Zone), where you'll find more restaurants and nightspots to choose from along Avenida Paseo de los Heroes. The city's cultural center is also located here, with its wraparound theatre, art exhibits, and bookstore. Just south of Paseo de los Heroes is Agua Caliente Boulevard where you'll find the bullring and race track. The Caliente Race Track has both thoroughbred and greyhound racing, and pari-mutual betting.

About forty-five minutes from the border is Rosarito Beach, where you can bargain at the roadside stands or sip a margarita at the Rosarito Beach Hotel. Fifteen minutes farther, and you'll come to Puerto Nuevo, where lobster is the local specialty at the many restaurants. Back on the highway toward Ensenada, stop in at La Fonda's, a roadside restaurant and inn. Dine on the outdoor terrace framed by bougainvillaea with a view of the broad sweep of beach below. Ensenada is an hour or so beyond, along a winding road with breathtaking views of the rocky coastline. The city bustles with activity. There are lots of shops to browse in, many offering high-quality Mexican handicrafts. Stop in at Hussong's, a bar that's a favorite among American tourists. And have a fish taco at the line of stands across from the fish market, while you watch the fishmongers feed greedy pelicans.

If you drive your own car across the border, it's a good idea to buy Mexican car insurance. If you're driving a rental car, check with the rental agency. Many prohibit taking rental cars across the border.

About the Author

Andrea Naversen is a writer and television newscaster based in San Diego. Most recently she served as an anchor and reporter at KFMB-TV, San Diego, where she covered the city's life and times for five years. Before coming to San Diego in 1988, she lived in Los Angeles for six years, working as a network correspondent for both CBS and ABC News. Her assignments for news shows, including "Good Morning America" and "World News Tonight," took her all over the United States, Europe, and the Middle East. She has also anchored ABC's "Newsbrief" and "Business Brief" on the West Coast, and ABC's "World News This Morning" in Washington DC.

Naversen began her journalism career as a reporter with *The Plain Dealer* in Cleveland, where she covered the police beat, courts, government, and education. After freelancing for *Time* and *Business Week*, she joined WTAE-TV in Pittsburgh, where she served as a general assignment reporter and headed the station's consumer investigative team.

Naversen is married to a commercial airline pilot who shares her love of travel.

About the Photographer

Kenneth Naversen—Andrea's older brother—is a freelance photographer who specializes in architectural and travel subjects. He is a recipient of an Art Critics Fellowship from the National Endowment for the Arts and holds a master's degree in Art and Photography. His work has appeared in numerous books and magazines, and he is the author as well as photographer of two previous titles for Beautiful America Publishing: *West Coast Victorians: A Nineteenth Century Legacy* and *East Coast Victorians: Cottages and Castles.*

Ranunculus gardens, Carlsbad

*Rear Cover: The **Star of India** at the Embarcadero*